P9-BVG-212

A BOOK OF CUT
FLOWERS

BY
SHEILA OKUN

ILLUSTRATIONS BY MARY CLOSE

A FRIEDMAN GROUP BOOK

Published by GALLERY BOOKS
An imprint of W.H. Smith Publishers, Inc.
112 Madison Avenue
New York, New York 10016

ISBN 0-8317-1891-9

A BOOK OF CUT FLOWERS
was prepared and produced by
Michael Friedman Publishing Group, Inc.
15 West 26th Street
New York, NY 10010

Typeset by B.P.E. Graphics, Inc.
Color separations by Hong Kong Scanner Craft Company Ltd.
Printed and bound in Hong Kong by Leefung-Asco Printers Ltd.

CONTENTS

INTRODUCTION

When my partner and I were studying landscape design, we hardly expected we would become florists. In those days—less than a decade ago—the average flower shop was three-fifths ferns and baby's-breath, one-fifth daisies and mums, and another fifth assorted roses, gladiolus, and corsage flowers. Only the rich could get bird-of-paradise and spray orchids, poppies and irises, and Rubrum lilies. All that has changed. Better distribution—chiefly from the gigantic flower markets near Amsterdam in Holland—has more than doubled the number of beautiful species readily available. Our International Flower Market, and other shops like it, show this change to advantage, selling as wide a variety of species as possible at a reasonable price per stem. The flowers are set out in the store for anyone to touch and smell. We do weddings, funerals, and other occasions, but we specialize in flowers for everyday enjoyment. We like to let people choose their own combinations and imagine their own arrangements. I have written this book to show just how wide and lovely a selection there is, and to give you a few ideas of how to use it.

Flower arranging is not nearly so difficult an art as some imagine. Most people have enough native good taste and familiarity with their environment to make pleasing and appropriate arrangements. As with any art, there are basic techniques which you need to know in order to begin.

When you purchase flowers, be sure that the ones you buy are fresh. To determine how fresh a flower is, look over the leaves. If they are turning yellow or spotting, it is a sure sign of age. Shaking a flower *gently* will also help you judge its freshness, since petals will fall if the flower is old. Try to buy flowers as close to bud stage as possible, since they will last longer. Buds will open up within a day if placed in warm water after being recut.

Any number of old wives' tales tell how to keep flowers fresh: recommendations include adding a pinch of sugar, two aspirin, or a penny to the water. None of these are effective. The best methods are to use floral preservative or a few drops of bleach or soda pop. Each acts as a bactericide. But perhaps the easiest way to keep flowers fresh is to start out with a clean container, change water daily, and frequently recut the stems.

When you have chosen your flowers and are ready to arrange them, prepare both stems and water. Cut the bottom of the stems with a sharp knife, not scissors, slicing on an angle to provide more surface for absorption of water. All foliage should be removed from the lower part of the stems, as otherwise it will decay and create bacteria in the water, clogging the stems and inhibiting their ability to draw water. All flowers—with the exception of irises, which must always be put in cold water—do best when placed in lukewarm water.

Healthy flowers aside, the most important element in any flower arrangement is the device that holds it together. Probably the most common and versatile of support devices is the pin holder, or frog. It can be found in all sizes and shapes, but the most practical sizes are those between two and three inches (3–8 cm) across. Waterproof clay, which is reusable, should be used to affix the pin holder to the bottom of the container.

Probably the next most popular holding aid is Oasis, or floral foam. It is sold in bricks or blocks in flower markets. Soaked for even a few minutes in water, it will supply moisture to the flower stems for several days. But note that some flowers with soft stems, such as gerberas and anemones, don't do well in Oasis: the tips of the stems become clogged.

Whether you use a pin holder or foam, place the stems as close together as possible without crowding them. Try to cut stems to unequal lengths or add ones of the same length at different angles so they don't all appear to be the same height. Additional interest can be gained by using flowers at different stages of development, particularly buds, and by facing the flowers in different directions.

One can also keep flowers in place by using wire netting. Chicken wire works well in tall containers and will support heavy stems. Once the wire is wedged inside the container, it can be left in place and reused. The most beautiful means for holding stems, particularly in glass containers, are small river rocks or pebbles, which add color and texture to the inside of the container and can be used to hide a pin holder. Clear glass marbles or chips look good used in the same way in contemporary designs.

Even the most unconventional or ultramodern arrangement in some way organizes the material and employs simple elements of design. Color commands attention most forcefully, so care should be taken to select materials of compatible hue. Line and pattern must also be considered. Balance is an integral part of the arrangement; it is established by the placement of the main stem, or vertical axis, and the relationship or distribution of the other flowers around it. Larger or darker flowers tend to establish weight at the base, where it belongs, and smaller, light-colored flowers may be placed higher up in a design.

Proportion is another factor that greatly influences the success of the arrangement: the height and width of the flowers should be one-and-one-half to two times that of the container. Although there are exceptions to this rule—it can be altered, for example, by extending the arrangement down the sides of the container—it's a good rule of thumb to use when deciding what quantity of flowers to buy.

Mass arrangements are typically full and contain a fair quantity of similar material. The flowers usually radiate from a central point, and the overall arrangement has a recognizable shape, such as round, triangular, or fan. The design evolves from the use of background materials, called "filler," chosen for their similarity, and striking flowers that are repeated to serve as focal points.

Modern art has a profound effect on flower arranging, and modern arrangements reflect this influence. Fewer flowers are used, and natural forms are altered by knotting, bending or clipping stems, foliage, and branches. Exaggerated proportions and exotic materials surprise the eye, and the bold forms and sharp contrasts excite interest.

Ikebana, or Japanese floral art, has also influenced flower arranging, especially modern designs. Though the use of plant material may be sparing, a sense of harmony prevails. Balance is based upon the Oriental *yin-yang* approach to the phenomena of nature and is very orderly and controlled. There are numerous schools of *ikebana*, such as Nagiere, Rikka, Shoka, and Moribana. The enthusiastic flower arranger can learn to experiment with classical *ikebana* or with one-, two-, or three-flower designs.

For both Western and Eastern design, another important consideration is foliage. Leaves, bare branches, and berry-covered branches are indispensable as filler to enhance your design. Consider lemon leaves, ti leaves, and the foliage of eucalyptus, pittosporum, and ruscus, in addition to the more traditional Baker and asparagus ferns. Experiment with different materials, and don't hesitate to pick up an interesting branch and prune it to suit your needs. First and last, flower arranging should be an expression of your own sense of fun and artistry.

Sheila Okun
New York

ACACIA

WATTLE

MIMOSA

(A. decurrens dealbata, A. longifolia)

(Family: *Leguminosae*)

The flowers on a stalk of acacia resemble a large
version of the blossoms of baby's-breath. The sunny,
yellow, ball-shaped flowers are small and fluffy and
have a dainty, ethereal quality. They look beautiful
with white or other yellow flowers. Available only for a
short time during the autumn, they are a good filler
flower or can be used by themselves as a striking
accent in a shiny black vase. Inexpensive and
relatively long-lived, they are a
delightful addition to any bouquet.

ALSTROEMERIA

PERUVIAN LILY
(A. pelegrina, A. aurantiaca)
(Family: *Liliaceae*)

Alstroemeria is hardly impressive in itself, but it is an exquisite and versatile flower for your arranging palette. Available in pink, apricot, salmon, red, lilac, yellow, and cream—streaked or dappled with white, green, or beige—its clustered flowers blend with virtually any partner. The unassertive, delicate trumpets set off more dramatic flowers like showy lilies, godetias, gerberas, or irises. Cheap, always available, and quite long-lived, it is among the most popular flowers in any market.

ANTHURIUM

FLAMINGO PLANT
(A. andreanum)
(Family: *Araceae*)

Once you have seen the anthurium, you will never confuse it with anything else. The Greek name means "tail flower," and it is easy to see why. The whitish "tail" is, in fact, composed of hundreds of tiny blossoms. When it is combined with the red, heart-shaped spathe, the total effect is so overwhelming that it is seldom possible to arrange anthuriums with any other flower. A bowl full of these tall exotics affixed to a frog or pin holder, makes a spectacular focal point for any room. Or, for a different effect, try using one or two of the flowers with such bold-textured foliage as palmetto or ti leaves to create a spare but compelling Oriental arrangement. Imported all year long from South America and Hawaii, anthuriums seem especially appropriate at Christmas.

ANTIRRHINUM

SNAPDRAGON
RABBIT'S MOUTH
(A. majus)
(Family: *Scrophulariaceae*)

Snapdragons evoke in almost everyone a fond nostalgia for childhood: Most of us recall pinching the blossoms along the stem to watch the "rabbit's mouth" open and close. Throughout the summer and fall, snapdragons are a popular favorite in flower markets because their long stems provide a good vertical axis for flower arrangements and their variety of colors (white, yellow, pink, orange, and burgundy) makes them among the most versatile of flowers. Snapdragons are not especially long-lived, but they are relatively inexpensive. It is difficult to imagine any "English garden" bouquet or arrangement without them.

ASTER

CHINA ASTER
(Callistephus chinensis)
(Family: *Compositae*)

For some reason, the flower that most florists and gardeners know as Aster is not really of the genus aster at all. The Callistephus, which everyone calls aster or China aster, comes in numerous varieties colored a vibrant purple, pink, or blue. All consist of a whorl of bright, coarse-textured petals set off around a yellow center. The flowers are plentiful during the summer and fall. They look wonderful combined with irises, snapdragons, marigolds, zinnias, or lilies. If the arrangement calls for a stiff, vertical form, make sure to wire the stem upright, since the head will nod otherwise.

BELLS OF IRELAND

MOLUCCA BALM
SHELL FLOWER
(Molucella laevis)
(Family: *Labiatae*)

The calyces and blooms of bells of Ireland together
make the flower. They do for each other what
diamond earrings do for ears. The actual blossoms
are tiny and white—barely visible at all—but, set in
green, bell-shaped calyces, they cluster strikingly up
and down the flower's long stem. Bells of Ireland are
long-lived and mix with other vertical forms, like
snapdragons and tuberoses. Because of their fresh,
green color, they can also be used instead of foliage
in a mass arrangement. For winter displays,
they can even be dried.

BIRD-OF-PARADISE

STRELITZIA
(S. reginae)
(Family: *Strelitziaceae*)

The exotic appearance of the bird-of-paradise makes
it a showy but versatile flower. The tall
stalk—straight and leafless—is topped by a large
purple-and-orange bloom resembling the head of a
tropical bird. For a stark, contemporary look, several
may be grouped in a tall, angular container. In a
more traditional arrangement, Strelitzia may be
combined with flowers of similar color, such as the
purple monkshood (aconitum) or the orange
strawflower. They can also be used in *ikebana,* for
even when the stems are cut short, "birds" make a
dramatic statement.

CENTAUREA

BACHELOR'S BUTTON
CORNFLOWER
BLUEBOTTLE
(C. cyanus)
(Family: *Compositae*)

Though cornflowers are available in pink, red, lavender, and white, the vibrance of its blue variety makes this bloom unmatched in popularity by any other blue flower. (Painters once used its pigment to make cyan blue.) The thin, leafy stems are covered with gray-green foliage and topped with a round, carnation-like flower. Available chiefly during the summer months—when it grows wild in grain fields around the world—cornflowers combine well with other flowers of medium height such as irises, daisies, snapdragons, and freesias.

CHRYSANTHEMUM

(C. hybrids)
(Family: *Compositae*)

All chrysanthemums originally came from China, Japan, or Korea, and the total number of hybrids available is huge. The Japanese prefer reflexed, or recurved, petals; the Chinese like them incurved. So central is the mum to Japanese culture that the country's flag represents it: The "rising sun" is really a sixteen-petal chrysanthemum.

Spider mums and exhibition mums are only the most striking florist's varieties of chrysanthemum. Those represented here are less able to stand alone, but they are among the finest and most versatile fillers for mass arrangements. The yellow pompoms provide concentrated bursts of color, while the so-called shasta daisy has true white petals, making it a natural for white-on-white arrangements. The larger hybrid mums shown here, while not as dramatic as some, are available in almost any color combination. They are reasonably priced and available all year long.

DAISY

MARGUERITE DAISY
OX-EYE CHAMOMILE
(Anthemis tinctoria)
(Family: *Compositae*)

Of all flowers, the daisy is perhaps the most cheerful, its white ray petals setting off a golden yellow center. Hardy and inexpensive, it is an excellent filler in mass arrangements and highlights informal bouquets of garden flowers. The foliage, which is deeply cut and sometimes fragrant, withers more quickly than the flower, so you can keep daisies longer if you remove the foliage when it no longer looks fresh. The Marguerite mixes with almost any other flower, but is especially beautiful with Mercedes roses.

DELPHINIUM

CANDLE-DELPHINIUM
CHINESE DELPHINIUM
(D. elatum, D. grandiflorum)
(Family: *Ranunculaceae*)

Only centaurea can match the intense blue found in
delphinium. Though there are white and pink
varieties, the light- and dark-blue shades are the
most attractive. They are so blue that people often
assume the flowers have been sprayed or dyed. The
lush stalks are covered with vibrant flowers whose
papery petals end in a long spur or tail which
protrudes from the back. Their genus name comes
from the Greek for "dolphin," a fish the flowers are
said to resemble. They look wonderful in naturalistic
country-garden arrangements with lilies, gerberas,
snapdragons, or stock, and they combine well in any
mixed bouquet where blue is needed.

DIANTHUS

CARNATIONS
(D. caryophyllus)
(Family: *Caryophyllaceae*)

The standard carnation is among the most
accessible, long-lived, and inexpensive flowers. At
one time or another, most buttonholes have been
graced with its vibrant colors and sweet scent.
Available in red, white, pink, and salmon shades, the
12- to 18-inch (30–45 cm) stems have a medium,
rounded flower head with slim, gray-green foliage.

EUPHORBIA

FLOWERING SPURGE
(E. fulgens)
(Family: *Euphorbiaceae*)

Euphorbia is related to poinsettia, the showy, red, flowering plant seen at Christmas, and they share a similar structure, though on a different scale. In both plants, what appear to be flower petals are really bright bracts (small leaves) which surround the tiny flower. Euphorbia cascades along willowy, arching branches, a habit that makes it very attractive in mass arrangements. The two- to three-foot (60–90 cm) stem is covered with tiny blossoms in white, yellow, or red. They look wonderful trailing gracefully down the sides of a tall ceramic container or a round woven basket. Don't hesitate to use them as filler in mass arrangements, since they mix well with virtually every other flower.

FREESIA

(F. refracta hybrids)
(Family: *Iridaceae*)

Freesia is the florist's most beautiful contradiction. Its light and diaphanous petals, found in saturated shades of lavender, pink, yellow, and white, stand upright in heavy bunches on a flower stalk that emerges from only one side of the stem. This club-footed delicacy comes with a rich, sweet scent that can fill a whole room with fragrance. Setting pairs of Freesia in a bud vase—say, beside the bed—is a pleasure in itself, since to arrange even numbers of the stems is to create do-it-yourself symmetry. And since the flowers are available all year long, one can mix them with almost any other bloom or use them as extenders in mass arrangements, always adding fragrance together with color. Though there may be between six and eight flowers on a stalk, often the smallest buds nearest the end are dormant, so don't expect all of them to bloom. Feel free to pinch off the first bloom, which will wither before the rest.

GLORIOSA ROTHSCHILD

GLORIOSA LILY
ROTHSCHILD LILY
(G. rothschildiana, G. superba)
(Family: *Liliaceae*)

Gloriosa lilies have a unique, contorted beauty that never becomes tiresome. Since they grow on vines, the slender stems are often twisted and the tips of the leaves curl like tendrils. The flowers are several inches in diameter, with waxy crimson and gold petals which are so inverted that the flower looks to be inside out. They make a startling arrangement with yellow oncidium orchids; otherwise, they are best displayed on their own in small, sparse arrangements or alone in bud vases.

GLADIOLUS

COLVILLE GLADIOLUS
MINI-GLADIOLUS
(Gladiolus x nanus)
(Family: *Iridaceae*)

There are hundreds of gladiolus hybrids, but the first of them—and perhaps the most dramatic—was the *nanus,* sometimes called *colvillei* or Colville gladiolus. Spiky and colorful like the rest of the genus, its stems are much shorter, usually only around 18 inches (45 cm), making it a natural for smaller-scale arrangements. Several varieties, such as the white "Nymph," have a lovely maroon diamond that extends into the flower's throat. Also available in pink, red, and salmon shades, these long-lived stems are often used as extenders in small settings. For a different effect, try them cut quite short and massed in a round container.

GYPSOPHILA

BABY'S-BREATH
(G. paniculata)
(Family: *Caryophyllaceae*)

Baby's-breath has been much overused;
consequently, it is much—and unjustly—maligned.
Many florists will still add a spray of gypsophila to
virtually any purchase, no matter how inappropriate,
so zealous connoisseurs will indignantly reject it.
Don't be too hasty. For those traditional, Edwardian
arrangements where a dainty, misty effect is called
for, baby's-breath is an ideal filler. The spider web of
twigs is covered with a profusion of tiny, white
blossoms which may even be dried for extended use.
A larger-flowered species, *G. elegans,* is a pleasant
compromise when you want delicacy without quite
the airy quality of baby's-breath.

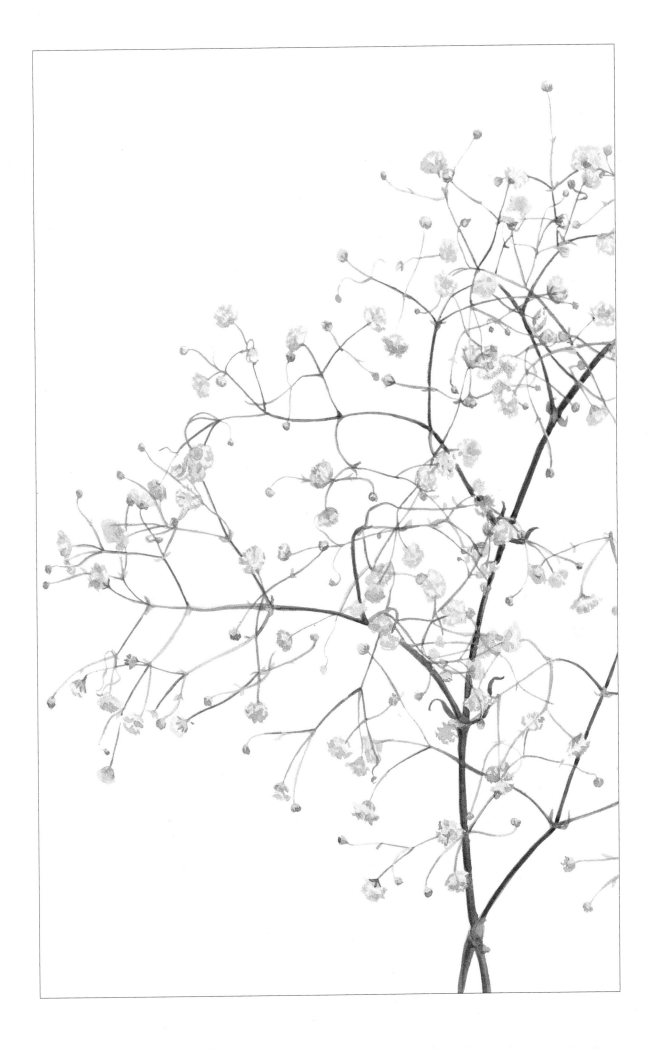

HELICHRYSUM

STRAWFLOWER
EVERLASTING FLOWER
CORNFLOWER
(H. bracteatum)
(Family: *Compositae*)

Strawflowers can be found in the summer,
but—fresh or dried—they are most popular during
the fall. Providentially, they share the colors of
autumn leaves—red, orange, gold, and purple—and
they retain their color as they dry. The stiff flower
heads are made up of whorls of tiny, pointed petals
usually enclosing a fuzzy, yellow corolla. Of medium
height, strawflowers look lovely in traditional
combinations with other dried materials: statice,
baby's-breath, cattails, and oak or maple leaves. To
dry the flowers, hang branches of them upside
down in a cool place.

IRIS

FLAG
(I. reticulata, I. xiphium)
(Family: *Iridaceae*)

It is said that the iris is the flower from which the form of the French *fleur de lis* was derived, and certainly there are few flowers which share the same graceful architectural form. Named for the Greek goddess of the rainbow, irises were thought to be flowers with a great variety of color, though today they are mainly available in shades of blue, lavender, yellow, or white. The swordlike foliage looks wonderful in Oriental designs, but the flower adapts well to mass arrangements as well as *ikebana.* The ten- to eighteen-inch (25–45 cm) stalks are crowned by a flower which has three upright standard petals and three horizontal or hanging falls which are often striped with yellow or purple. Some even have a fuzzy ridge or crest and are known as bearded iris. They are inexpensive and available throughout the year, but they are not long-lived.

LILAC

MAY
(Syringa Vulgaris)
(Family: *Oleaceae*)

Lilacs are available for such a short time—May and June only—that a chance to buy them should never be missed. Nothing has quite the same sweet fragrance, lush blossoms, or pleasant associations. In parts of Devonshire, they are simply called May. They are usually sold in bunches for quite inexpensive sums, so treat yourself when you can. Rather than combining them with other flowers, fill a bowl with nothing but two- to three-foot (60–90 cm) lilac stems and watch the faces light up as people enter the room. Fairly long-lived, lilacs have masses of tiny single or double blue, lavender, or white blossoms, and heart-shaped leaves. The Greek generic name means "flute," for the branches of lilac were once used to make them.

LILIUM

CONNECTICUT KING & RED KNIGHT
(L. hybrids)
(Family: *Liliaceae*)

The hybrid lilies are commanding beauties, their colors vibrant and saturated, their blooms firm, recurved, and symmetrical, and their unopened blossoms arrayed with a regal carelessness. Among the longest-lived of all cut flowers, they can be found in every color except blue and purple, at virtually any time of year. Varieties range in height from two to five feet (60–150 cm) and may have as few as two or as many as five flowers per stem. Two hybrids are most sought after for the purity of their hues: the yellow Connecticut King and the crimson Red Knight. Lilies are seldom cheap, but you can hardly go wrong when you buy them. They look lovely alone or in virtually any color-compatible combination.

LILIUM

RUBRUM LILY
(L. speciosum 'Rubrum')
(Family: *Liliaceae*)

As wonderful as all lilies may be, the Rubrum is in a class by itself. It is the Rolls Royce of lilies, the Mick Jagger, the "Dr. J." A variety called Uchida has stems five feet long (150 cm), covered with buds and pendulous white flowers speckled with maroon in their throats. They give the effect of a group of dancers in mid-jump. Other members of the family—Star Gazers, Dominiques, or Mercy lilies—have shorter stems and a more solid feminine beauty, the large flowers (up to six inches, 15 cm, across) are tinged with a pink-and-maroon center. The pollen-coated anthers that emerge from the flower will indeed drop the orange pollen after a little while, so some people cut the anthers off. The flower itself will stay firm for ten days or even two weeks. Mix Rubrums with red or pink roses, gerberas, stock, delphiniums, or monkshood.

LIMONIUM

STATICE
SEA LAVENDER
(L. sinuatum)
(Family: *Plumbaginaceae*)

Although the natural home of sea lavender, or statice,
is the meadow or salt marsh, it is cultivated as a cut
flower because it is so versatile and long-lived. Statice
grows on an erect, winged stalk, with clusters of tiny
flowers which, like freesia, rise at right angles from
their stems. Sold throughout the year, it is available
in white, blue, lavender, or pink. Statice is often used
as filler in mass arrangements instead of
baby's-breath because it has more body but still
transmits a light, airy feeling. Excellent as a dried
flower, it combines well with strawflowers
and miniature cattails.

MONKSHOOD

WOLF'S-BANE
(Aconitum napellus)
(Family: *Ranunculaceae*)

The deadly juice of monkshood was once used as a sedative and even for arrow poison, but we value the plant today for its delicate ornamental flower. The blossom has a rich, blue color and a hooded shape, while the foliage—dark green and deeply cut—has ornamental value in itself. The flower's long spikes are two to three feet (60–90 cm) high with numerous small flowers all along the stem. It arranges well with other tall flowers such as bird-of-paradise, lilies, snapdragons, and mums. Fairly long-lived, monkshood is available throughout the spring and summer.

PHYSALIS

CHINESE LANTERNS
WINTER CHERRY
(P. alkekengi, P. franchetti)
(Family: *Solanaceae*)

Unlike most cut flowers, physalis is not valued for its flower or its foliage but earns its popularity for the pleasing shape and vibrant color of its seed pod. The bright orange seed coverings look like miniature Chinese lanterns as they dangle delicately from the branches on small, arching stems. Usually the florist will remove the foliage for you, to give the "lanterns" maximum visibility. The stems are over a foot long (30 cm), so they make wonderful extenders in autumn arrangements, combined with either fresh-cut or dried flowers. Chinese lanterns themselves can be dried and used over and over again.

PINCUSHION FLOWER

SCABIOSA
(S. caucasica, S. atropururea)
(Family: *Dipsaceae*)

Scabiosa was once thought to cure itching—hence its
unattractive generic name—but today we value it for
its fragile flower. Its parchment petals, sweet
fragrance, and longevity make the pincushion flower
a popular favorite. The flowers range in color from
one sort which is nearly black to one which is white,
but the most common colors are blue, pink, lavender,
salmon, and red. The ruffled petals
spread like a petticoat around a center of silvery
stamens which look like a pincushion, giving the
flower its common name. Of medium height,
scabiosas are ideal matches for irises, Rubrum lilies,
and shasta daisies.

ROSES

(Rosa hybrids)
(Family: *Rosaceae*)

There is scarcely a culture in the world that doesn't know the rose. The most important discoveries made about roses in recent years, apart from hybridization, have to do with their care: The annoying tendency of cut roses to nod on the stem can be prevented by recutting the stems *under water.* Another, more traditional way to prolong the life of a rose is to avoid exposing it to direct sunlight or heat.

Excellent red roses are the American Beauty (top), which has a lovely scent and a clear red color, and the Mercedes (bottom left), with its cabbage-shaped head, bright orange-red color, and outstanding longevity. Sonia (top left) is the most well known and attractive of the roses in the pink or peach family. The Sweetheart rose (bottom right), a small-flowered, short-stemmed variety, is inexpensive and lends itself well to mixed arrangements. Yellow and white roses are also good mixers. Try white roses in arrangements with other whites: tuberoses, baby's-breath, or shasta daisies.

STOCK

BROMPTON STOCK
(Mathiola incana)
(Family: *Cruciferae*)

The pungent, spicy aroma of stock evokes visions of evening in an Oriental paradise. The fragrance seems to increase as the sun goes down. The richly scented flowers—available in purple, lavender, or white—grow on woody stalks with the blossoms massed toward the top. Available primarily during the summer months, it is fairly long-lived. To preserve stock a bit longer, smash the bottom of the stems instead of cutting them.

THISTLE

GLOBE THISTLE & SCOTCH THISTLE
(Echinops ritro & Onopordon bracteatum)
(Family: *Compositae*)

Globe thistle makes a dynamic display. As it ages, it seems to increase in interest. The medium, gray-blue flower head is cut while the myriad tiny blossoms that comprise its head are in bud; as they open, the tight iridescent ball of blue becomes an eye-catching cluster. The stems are of medium height and the leaves are a shiny green with a spiny texture. The Onopordon, or Scotch thistle, has a more elongated, globular head with eerie, sinuous tentacles surrounding it. Thistles retain their attractive appearance when dried, so hold on to them for dried as well as fresh-cut arrangements.

TUBEROSE

POLIANTHES
(P. tuberosa)
(Family: *Agavaceae*)

Tuberoses are without exception the most fragrant of all flowers sold. Perhaps the most odorous rose is sweeter, but you won't find it in the flower market. As a matter of fact, the essential oils from specially selected hybrids of both tuberoses and roses are used to make costly perfumes. Both double- and single-flower tuberoses are scented. The double flower, which is white with a pink tinge, has a much stiffer vertical habit, while the pure white single variety tends to nod. Both varieties are medium-tall, covered with lovely jasminelike blossoms; both will last for a week or more and can be bought throughout the year. They are expensive, but you need only a few to turn a bouquet into a sweet delight.

YARROW

ACHILLEA
(A. filipendulina)
(Family: *Compositae*)

Yarrow has a modern, minimalist beauty that lends itself to both mass and sparse Oriental arrangements. A group of yarrow looks like a tiny grove of tropical trees. The long, arrow-straight stem has attractive fernlike leaves and mustard-colored flowers that group in quiltlike mounds at the top of the stalk. Yarrow dries perfectly and looks best when combined with fresh or dried strawflowers and statice.

ZANTEDESCHIA

CALLA LILY
ARUM LILY
LILY OF THE NILE
(Z. aethiopica)
(Family: *Araceae*)

The large, trumpet-shaped blossom of the calla lily is
pristine-white. Some specimens give the effect of
blown glass; others, of porcelain or polished marble.
From the center of the sinuous petal—perhaps to
keep the flower from taking itself *too* seriously—rises
a bright yellow spadix. All of this seriocomic display
is propped on a stout stem over two feet (60 cm) high.
Callas are such an event in themselves that it is
difficult to think of combining them with other
flowers, but, if you must, keep the arrangement stark
and architectural or sparse and Oriental.

ZINNIAS

Youth-and-Age
(Z. elegans)
(Family: *Compositae*)

Zinnias are among the most common garden flowers, blooming from early summer to late autumn. They are also excellent cut flowers and should not be missed. Zinnias come in yellow, orange, red, and pink, with multicolored and striped varieties. The large flowers have slightly coarse but vibrantly colored petals in both single and double varieties. Zinnias are best for informal country bouquets or arrangements, combined with chrysanthemums, irises, or statice.